snazzy snacks

THE AUSTRALIAN
Women's Weekly

CONTENTS

recipes 4
  snacks-on-the-run 12
  bites 20
  skewers 32
  dips 42
  sandwiches & rolls 56
  sandwiches & wraps 70
  melts & bruschetta 72
glossary 74
conversion chart 77
index 78

AUSTRALIAN CUP AND SPOON MEASUREMENTS ARE METRIC. A CONVERSION CHART APPEARS ON PAGE 77.

Whether feeding the family or catering for guests, these snazzy snacks will hit the spot. They're great if you just want a light bite to take the edge off mid-afternoon hunger, or for an after-school snack for the kids. And the recipes also double as a selection of finger food when entertaining, ending the age old problem of what to serve guests.

Pamela Clark

Food Director

melon in prosciutto

CHILLI SALT PRAWNS

prep & cook time 20 minutes serves 4 nutritional count
per serving 10.9g total fat (2.7g saturated fat); 991kJ
(237 cal); 5.5g carbohydrate; 29.1g protein; 0.2g fibre

1kg uncooked medium king prawns
1 tablespoon olive oil
2 teaspoons sea salt flakes
½ teaspoon dried chilli flakes
1 teaspoon finely chopped fresh
    flat-leaf parsley
yogurt dipping sauce
1 cup (280g) yogurt
2 tablespoons mayonnaise
1 tablespoon finely grated lemon rind
1 tablespoon lemon juice

1 Preheat oven to 220°C/200°C fan-forced.
Oil oven tray; line with baking paper.
2 Shell and devein prawns, leaving tails intact.
3 Combine prawns, oil, salt and chilli on tray;
spread prawns into single layer. Cook prawns
about 10 minutes.
4 Meanwhile, make yogurt dipping sauce.
5 Sprinkle parsley over sauce; serve dipping
sauce with prawns.
yogurt dipping sauce Combine ingredients in
small bowl.

MELON IN PROSCIUTTO

prep time 20 minutes serves 4 nutritional count
per serving 11.9g total fat (2.2g saturated fat); 802kJ
(192 cal); 10.9g carbohydrate; 9.4g protein; 2.5g fibre

1 small rockmelon (1.3kg), halved lengthways
12 thin slices prosciutto (180g)
2 tablespoons extra virgin olive oil
¼ cup fresh flat-leaf parsley leaves

1 Peel and seed rockmelon; cut into 12 wedges.
2 Wrap one prosciutto slice around each
melon wedge, place on serving platter; drizzle
with oil, sprinkle with parsley.

chilli salt prawns

PORK DUMPLINGS

prep & cook time 40 minutes makes 40 nutritional count per dumpling 0.2g total fat (0g saturated fat); 63kJ (15 cal); 0.6g carbohydrate; 2.5g protein; 0g fibre

250g pork mince
½ cup (40g) finely chopped wombok
2 green onions, chopped finely
2 tablespoons finely chopped fresh
  garlic chives
2cm piece fresh ginger (10g), grated
2 teaspoons light soy sauce
2 teaspoons cornflour
40 wonton wrappers
sweet soy dipping sauce
¼ cup (60ml) light soy sauce
2 teaspoons white vinegar
2 teaspoons brown sugar

1 Combine pork, wombok, onion, chives, ginger, sauce and cornflour in medium bowl; season.

2 Place 1 level teaspoon of the pork mixture into centre of each wonton wrapper; brush edges with a little water, pinch edges together to seal.

3 Place dumplings, in batches, in large baking-paper-lined bamboo steamer. Steam, covered, over large saucepan of boiling water about 4 minutes or until cooked through.

4 Meanwhile, combine ingredients for sweet soy dipping sauce in small bowl. Serve dumplings with dipping sauce.

VEGETABLE RICE PAPER ROLLS

prep time 35 minutes makes 24 nutritional count
per roll 0.2g total fat (0g saturated fat); 92kJ (22cal);
3.9g carbohydrate; 0.8g protein; 0.6g fibre

1 large carrot (180g), grated coarsely
2 stalks celery (300g), trimmed,
    chopped finely
150g wombok, shredded finely
2 teaspoons fish sauce
2 teaspoons brown sugar
1 tablespoon lemon juice
24 x 17cm-square rice paper sheets
24 fresh mint leaves

1 Combine carrot, celery, wombok, sauce, sugar and juice in small bowl; season to taste.
2 Place 1 sheet of rice paper in medium bowl of warm water until just softened; carefully lift sheet from water, placing it on a clean tea towel with a corner pointing towards you. Place 1 level tablespoon of the vegetable mixture horizontally in centre of sheet; top with 1 mint leaf. Fold corner facing you over filling; roll rice paper to enclose filling, folding in sides after first complete turn of roll. Repeat to make a total of 24 rolls.

note If not serving rolls immediately, place, seam-side down, on a plastic-wrap-lined tray; cover with damp paper towel and refrigerate until ready to serve.

best-ever chicken sandwiches

BEST-EVER CHICKEN SANDWICHES

prep & cook time **25 minutes (+ standing)** makes **4**
nutritional count per sandwich **31g total fat**
(9.6g saturated fat); 2658kJ (636 cal);
47.8g carbohydrate; 40.2g protein; 3g fibre

600g chicken breast fillets
½ cup (150g) mayonnaise
¼ cup coarsely chopped fresh
    flat-leaf parsley
8 slices white sandwich bread (360g)
40g butter, softened

1 Place chicken in medium saucepan; add
enough cold water to cover. Bring to the boil,
reduce heat; simmer 10 minutes. Remove
from heat. Stand 30 minutes; drain.
2 Cut chicken into 2cm pieces; combine in
medium bowl with mayonnaise and parsley.
Season to taste.
3 Spread bread with butter; sandwich chicken
mixture between bread slices. Cut sandwiches
into triangles.

note The chicken mixture can be made a day ahead,
keep refrigerated. Use a whole-egg mayonnaise for the
creamiest-tasting filling.

Vegemite cheese straws

VEGEMITE CHEESE STRAWS

prep & cook time **30 minutes** makes **24** nutritional count
per straw **1g total fat (0.5g saturated fat); 67kJ**
(16 cal); 0.6g carbohydrate; 1.1g protein; 0g fibre

2 sheets puff pastry
1 tablespoon Vegemite
⅔ cup (50g) grated parmesan cheese

1 Preheat oven to 220°C/200°C fan-forced. Oil
oven trays; line with baking paper.
2 Spread one pastry sheet with half the
Vegemite; sprinkle with half the cheese. Top
with remaining pastry sheet; spread with
remaining Vegemite, then sprinkle with
remaining cheese.
3 Cut pastry stack in half; place one stack on
top of the other, press down firmly. Cut pastry
crossways into 24 strips; twist each strip,
pinching ends to seal. Place on trays; bake
about 12 minutes or until browned lightly.

ORANGE AND HONEY NUT MIX

prep & cook time **30 minutes (+ cooling)** makes **3 cups**
nutritional count per ½ cup **35g total fat**
(4.5g saturated fat); 1885kJ (451 cal);
18.9g carbohydrate; 14.3g protein; 5.3g fibre

Preheat oven to 180°C/160°C fan-forced.
Combine 1 cup raw unsalted cashews, 1 cup
raw unsalted peanuts, 1 cup raw almond kernels,
1 tablespoon finely grated orange rind and
¼ cup honey in large bowl. Spread mixture
onto baking-paper-lined oven tray; cook,
stirring occasionally, about 20 minutes or until
crunchy. Cool mixture, stirring occasionally to
prevent clumping.

WARM ORANGE & FENNEL OLIVES

prep & cook time **10 minutes** serves **6** nutritional count
per serving **16.4g total fat (2.3g saturated fat); 866kJ**
(207 cal); 10.9g carbohydrate; 0.4g protein; 0.7g fibre

Peel thin strips of rind from 1 orange. Combine
rind with 400g mixed marinated seeded olives,
½ cup dry red wine, 1 teaspoon coarsely
ground black pepper and ½ teaspoon fennel
seeds in medium saucepan; bring to a simmer.
Stand 10 minutes before serving warm.

SNACKS-ON-THE-RUN

HOT AND SPICY POPCORN

prep & cook time **20 minutes** makes **12 cups**
nutritional count per ½ cup **4.6g total fat**
(1.4g saturated fat); 209kJ (50 cal);
1.7g carbohydrate; 0.4g protein; 0.7g fibre

Cook ½ cup popping corn with ⅓ cup vegetable
oil in heated large saucepan, covered, shaking
pan occasionally, until corn stops popping;
place in large bowl. Add 40g melted butter,
1 teaspoon cayenne pepper, 1 teaspoon paprika
and 2 teaspoons sea salt; toss well.

FRUIT AND CEREAL SNACK

prep & cook time **20 minutes (+ cooling)** makes **3½ cups**
nutritional count per ¼ cup **3.6g total fat**
(3.1g saturated fat); 322kJ (77 cal);
9.7g carbohydrate; 0.7g protein; 2.1g fibre

Preheat oven to 180°C/160°C fan-forced.
Combine ½ cup rice bubbles, ½ cup cornflakes
and 1 cup flaked coconut in large shallow baking
dish; roast, uncovered, about 5 minutes, stirring
occasionally. Transfer to large bowl; cool. Stir in
½ cup finely chopped dried pear, ⅓ cup finely
chopped dried apple, ¼ cup finely chopped
seeded prunes and ½ cup dried cranberries.

lemon pepper chicken drumettes

CORN CAKES WITH AVOCADO SMASH

prep & cook time 30 minutes serves 8 nutritional count per serving 10.5g total fat (3.1g saturated fat); 769kJ (184 cal); 14.4g carbohydrate; 6g protein; 3.7g fibre

2 corn cobs (800g), trimmed
2 teaspoons olive oil
3 green onions, sliced thinly
2 tablespoons self-raising flour
¼ teaspoon bicarbonate of soda
2 eggs, beaten lightly
⅓ cup (80ml) light sour cream
avocado smash
1 medium avocado (250g), chopped coarsely
1 tablespoon lime juice

1 Cut kernels from corn cobs.
2 Heat oil in large frying pan; cook corn and onion, stirring, until onion softens. Cool.
3 Combine corn mixture, sifted flour and soda, and egg in medium bowl.
4 Heat oiled large frying pan, drop rounded tablespoons of mixture, in batches, into pan; cook about 1 minute each side.
5 Make avocado smash.
6 Serve corn cakes topped with smash and sour cream.

avocado smash Combine ingredients in small bowl; mash with fork; season to taste.

LEMON PEPPER CHICKEN DRUMETTES

prep & cook time 50 minutes serves 8 nutritional count per serving 9g total fat (2.5g saturated fat); 835kJ (199 cal); 0.1g carbohydrate; 29.2g protein; 0g fibre

16 chicken drumettes (1kg)
1 teaspoon finely grated lemon rind
2 tablespoons lemon juice
1 teaspoon cracked black pepper
1 tablespoon olive oil
¼ teaspoon ground turmeric
¼ teaspoon sweet paprika

1 Preheat oven to 200°C/180°C fan-forced. Line large baking dish with baking paper.
2 Combine ingredients in medium bowl; season.
3 Place chicken, in single layer, in dish; bake, uncovered, about 40 minutes or until cooked through. Cool.

note Chicken can be cooked, cooled and refrigerated a day ahead.

corn cakes with avocado smash

CHICKEN LIVER PÂTÉ

prep & cook time 45 minutes (+ refrigeration) makes 4 cups
nutritional count per teaspoon 1.7g total fat
(1g saturated fat); 88kJ (21 cal);
0.1g carbohydrate; 1.2g protein; 0g fibre

1kg chicken livers
200g ghee
4 rindless bacon rashers (260g)
1 small brown onion (80g), chopped finely
¼ cup (60ml) brandy
½ cup (125ml) cream
2 teaspoons finely chopped fresh thyme
pinch ground nutmeg

1 Cut any sinew from livers; pull each lobe away from connecting tissue.

2 Heat a quarter of the ghee in large frying pan; cook half the livers, stirring, until browned and barely cooked. Remove from pan. Repeat with another quarter of the ghee and remaining livers.

3 Heat 1 tablespoon of the remaining ghee in same pan; cook bacon and onion, stirring, until onion softens. Add brandy; bring to the boil.

4 Blend livers, bacon mixture, cream, thyme, nutmeg and 2 tablespoons of the remaining ghee until smooth (you may need to do this in batches).

5 Press pâté into 1-litre (4-cup) dish; melt remaining ghee, pour over pâté. Refrigerate 3 hours or overnight.

Serve with melba toasts or water crackers.

PEA AND PANCETTA FRITTATAS

prep & cook time 30 minutes makes 36 nutritional count per frittata 3.8g total fat (2.1g saturated fat); 178kJ (43 cal); 0.4g carbohydrate; 1.9g protein; 0.1g fibre

1 teaspoon olive oil
4 slices pancetta (60g), chopped finely
1 clove garlic, crushed
6 eggs
⅔ cup (160ml) cream
½ cup (60g) frozen peas
⅓ cup (25g) grated parmesan cheese
1 tablespoon finely chopped fresh mint
1 teaspoon finely grated lemon rind
2 tablespoons crème fraîche
36 small fresh mint leaves

1 Preheat oven to 200°C/180°C fan-forced. Grease three 12-hole (1-tablespoon/20ml) mini muffin pans.
2 Heat oil in small frying pan; cook pancetta and garlic, stirring, until pancetta is crisp. Cool.
3 Whisk eggs and cream in large jug; stir in pancetta mixture, peas, cheese, mint and rind. Season to taste. Pour egg mixture into pan holes.
4 Bake frittatas about 12 minutes or until set. Stand in pan 5 minutes before serving topped with crème fraîche and mint leaves.

BLUE CHEESE AND FIG BITES

prep & cook time **20 minutes** makes **12** nutritional count
per bite **11.9g total fat (2.9g saturated fat); 1012kJ
(242 cal); 25.5g carbohydrate; 6.2g protein; 3.9g fibre**

Process ⅓ cup roasted slivered almonds with
2 coarsely chopped green onions, 1 cup loosely
packed fresh mint leaves, ⅓ cup olive oil and
1 tablespoon lemon juice until smooth; season
to taste. Halve 1 long turkish loaf lengthways;
cut each half lengthways into 3 fingers then
cut fingers crossways into four to get 24 slices.
Toast bread under hot grill. Spread almond
mixture on half the toasts; top with 200g thinly
sliced semi-dried figs and 100g thinly sliced blue
cheese. Top with remaining toast; serve warm.

CAPRESE TARTLETS

prep & cook time **30 minutes** makes **9** nutritional count
per tartlet **4.5g total fat (2.1g saturated fat); 247kJ
(59 cal); 1.3g carbohydrate; 3.2g protein; 0.4g fibre**

Preheat oven to 220°C/200°C fan-forced. Cut
nine 7cm rounds from 1 sheet shortcrust pastry.
Place rounds on baking-paper-lined oven tray;
pierce with fork. Bake about 10 minutes. Spread
rounds with 2 tablespoons basil pesto. Top
rounds with 9 thinly sliced cherry tomatoes and
9 thinly sliced cherry bocconcini cheese; season
to taste. Bake about 2 minutes or until cheese
softens. Top each tartlet with a baby basil leaf.

CARAMELISED TOMATO AND HAM BITES

prep & cook time **40 minutes** makes **16** nutritional count per bite **7.5g total fat (4.1g saturated fat); 644kJ (154 cal); 12.7g carbohydrate; 8.4g protein; 0.7g fibre**

Cook 2 finely chopped shallots in heated oiled medium frying pan until soft. Add 250g halved cherry tomatoes; cook 5 minutes. Add ¼ cup balsamic vinegar and 1 tablespoon brown sugar; cook, stirring occasionally, until thickened, season to taste. Cut 1 brioche loaf into 16 slices; cut 32 x 6.5cm rounds from slices. Top half the slices with 2 cups grated pecorino cheese; grill until cheese melts. Toast remaining rounds until golden. Divide 185g thinly sliced double smoked leg ham among toast rounds; top each with caramelised tomatoes, top with remaining toasts. Serve warm.

BRIE AND QUINCE MATCHSTICKS

prep & cook time **20 minutes** makes **10** nutritional count per matchstick **7.7g total fat (4.7g saturated fat); 376kJ (90 cal); 0.6g carbohydrate; 4.9g protein; 0g fibre**

Preheat oven to 220°C/200°C fan-forced. Cut 1 sheet puff pastry into ten 12cm x 4.5cm rectangles. Cut 250g wedge brie cheese into 10 slices. Place pastry rectangles on lightly greased oven trays; pierce with fork. Bake about 10 minutes. Top hot matchsticks with cheese, a little quince paste and a lemon thyme sprig. Serve warm.

pizza muffins

PIZZA MUFFINS

prep & cook time 45 minutes makes 12 nutritional count
per muffin 11.8g total fat (6.1g saturated fat); 928kJ
(222 cal); 17g carbohydrate; 10.7g protein; 2.9g fibre

4 rindless bacon rashers (260g),
    chopped finely
4 green onions, chopped finely
2 cups (300g) self-raising flour
80g butter, melted
1 egg
1 cup (250ml) buttermilk
3 slices (120g) bottled roasted red capsicum,
    chopped finely
¾ cup (75g) pizza cheese
½ teaspoon dried chilli flakes

1 Preheat oven to 200°C/180°C fan-forced.
Grease 12-hole (⅓-cup/80ml) muffin pan.
2 Cook bacon in heated medium frying pan,
stirring, until browned lightly. Add onion; cook,
stirring, until onion softens. Cool.
3 Meanwhile, sift flour into medium bowl; stir
in combined butter, egg and buttermilk.
4 Add capsicum, cheese, chilli and bacon
mixture to buttermilk mixture; stir gently to
combine. Do not over-mix; mixture should
be lumpy.
5 Divide mixture among pan holes. Bake, in
oven, about 20 minutes. Stand muffins in pan
5 minutes before turning, top-side up, onto wire
rack. Serve muffins warm, plain or with butter.

baked ricotta

BAKED RICOTTA

prep & cook time 40 minutes (+ refrigeration) serves 8
nutritional count per serving 17g total fat
(6.5g saturated fat); 986kJ (236 cal);
10.7g carbohydrate; 10g protein; 0.9g fibre

500g fresh ricotta cheese
2 garlic cloves, chopped finely
½ teaspoon dried chilli flakes
½ teaspoon fresh thyme leaves
2 tablespoons grated parmesan cheese
2 tablespoons olive oil
120g packet flatbread
90g jar tomato tapenade

1 Press ricotta into 12cm sieve; place over
bowl, cover. Refrigerate 4 hours or overnight.
2 Preheat oven to 180°C/160°C fan-forced.
Grease oven tray, line with baking paper.
3 Turn ricotta onto tray; sprinkle with garlic,
chilli, thyme and parmesan, drizzle with oil.
Bake, uncovered, about 30 minutes or until
cheese is browned lightly. Cool.
4 Serve ricotta with flatbread and tomato
tapenade.

FISH AND CAPER CROQUETTES

prep & cook time 40 minutes (+ refrigeration) makes 16
nutritional count per croquette 7.9g total fat
(2.6g saturated fat); 573kJ (137 cal);
7.2g carbohydrate; 7.2g protein; 0.6g fibre

¾ cup (180ml) water
¾ cup (180ml) dry white wine
2 bay leaves
400g firm white fish fillets
40g butter
¼ cup (35g) plain flour
1 cup (250ml) milk
2 teaspoons finely grated lemon rind
2 tablespoons rinsed, drained baby capers,
   chopped finely
1 clove garlic, crushed
1 tablespoon finely chopped fresh chives
¼ cup (35g) plain flour, extra
1 egg, beaten lightly
1 cup (70g) stale breadcrumbs
vegetable oil, for shallow-frying
1 medium lemon, sliced thickly

1 Combine the water, wine and bay leaves in small saucepan; bring to the boil. Add fish, reduce heat; simmer, covered, about 5 minutes or until fish is cooked through. Drain fish; discard cooking liquid, flake fish coarsely.
2 Meanwhile, melt butter in medium saucepan. Add flour; cook, stirring, about 2 minutes or until mixture thickens and bubbles. Gradually stir in milk; cook, stirring, until mixture boils and thickens. Remove from heat; stir in rind, capers, garlic, chives and fish. Season to taste. Cover; refrigerate 2 hours.
3 Roll rounded tablespoons of fish mixture into ovals; coat in extra flour, shake off excess. Dip croquettes in egg then breadcrumbs.
4 Heat oil in large frying pan; cook croquettes until browned all over. Drain on absorbent paper. Serve with lemon slices.

bolognese turnovers

BOLOGNESE TURNOVERS

prep & cook time 45 minutes makes 16 nutritional
count per turnover 5g total fat (2g saturated fat); 364kJ
(87 cal); 3.4g carbohydrate; 6.8g protein; 0.5g fibre

2 teaspoons olive oil
1 small brown onion (80g), chopped finely
1 clove garlic, crushed
500g beef mince
2 tablespoons tomato paste
⅔ cup (170g) bottled tomato pasta sauce
⅓ cup finely chopped fresh flat-leaf parsley
4 sheets shortcrust pastry
1 egg, beaten lightly

1 Preheat oven to 200°C/180°C fan-forced.
Oil oven trays.
2 Heat oil in large frying pan; cook onion and
garlic, stirring, until onion softens. Add beef;
cook, stirring, until beef is cooked through. Add
paste and sauce; cook, stirring, until heated
through. Remove from heat; stir in parsley.
Season to taste.
3 Cut 16 x 11.5cm rounds from pastry. Spoon
¼ cup beef mixture into centre of each round.
Brush edges with a little egg; fold rounds in half
to enclose filling, pinch edges to seal.
4 Place turnovers on trays; brush with egg.
Bake about 15 minutes or until browned.

prawn cocktails

PRAWN COCKTAILS

prep time 30 minutes serves 4 nutritional count
per serving 14.2g total fat (4.2g saturated fat); 1254kJ
(300 cal); 7.6g carbohydrate; 34.6g protein; 1.8g fibre

32 cooked medium prawns (1.5g)
⅓ cup (100g) mayonnaise
2 tablespoons cream
1 tablespoon tomato sauce
1 teaspoon worcestershire sauce
½ teaspoon Tabasco sauce
½ teaspoon dijon mustard
2 teaspoons lemon juice
½ iceberg lettuce, shredded finely
4 lemon wedges

1 Shell and devein prawns.
2 Whisk mayonnaise, cream, sauces, mustard
and juice in small bowl; season to taste.
3 Divide lettuce among serving glasses; top
with prawns and sauce. Serve with lemon.

TERIYAKI CHICKEN RICE PAPER ROLLS

prep & cook time **40 minutes (+ refrigeration)** makes **24**
nutritional count per roll **3g total fat**
(0.9g saturated fat); 284kJ (68 cal);
3.5g carbohydrate; 6.5g protein; 0.7g fibre

6 chicken thigh fillets (660g), trimmed
¼ cup (60ml) thick teriyaki marinade
2 tablespoons water
2 lebanese cucumbers (260g)
2 teaspoons peanut oil
24 x 17cm-square rice paper sheets
200g enoki mushrooms, trimmed

1 Slice each chicken thigh lengthways into eight strips. Combine chicken, teriyaki and the water in small bowl, cover; refrigerate 1 hour. Drain chicken; discard marinade.

2 Cut cucumbers in half lengthways; discard seeds. Cut cucumber halves in half crossways; cut pieces into three strips lengthways.

3 Heat oil in large frying pan; cook chicken, in batches, until cooked through. Cool 10 minutes.

4 Place 1 sheet of rice paper in medium bowl of warm water until just softened; lift sheet carefully from water, placing it on a clean tea towel with a corner pointing towards you. Place two pieces of chicken horizontally in centre of rice paper; top with one piece of cucumber then a few mushrooms. Fold corner facing you over filling; roll rice paper to enclose filling, folding in one side after first complete turn of roll. Repeat to make a total of 24 rolls.

note **If not serving rolls immediately, place, seam-side down, on a plastic-wrap-lined tray; cover with damp paper towel and refrigerate until ready to serve.**

sweet potato crisps with chilli salt

SWEET POTATO CRISPS WITH CHILLI SALT

prep & cook time 25 minutes serves 4 nutritional count per serving 13.2g total fat (1.6g saturated fat); 1254kJ (300 cal); 38.7g carbohydrate; 4.4g protein; 4.8g fibre

1 medium kumara (400g)
1 medium white sweet potato (400g)
1 medium purple sweet potato (400g)
vegetable oil, for deep-frying
2 teaspoons sea salt flakes
½ teaspoon dried chilli flakes
½ teaspoon sweet paprika

1 Using vegetable peeler, slice vegetables into long, thin strips.
2 Heat oil in wok; deep-fry kumara and sweet potato strips, in batches, until browned lightly and crisp. Drain on wire rack over absorbent-paper-lined tray.
3 Combine salt, chilli and paprika in small bowl. Sprinkle hot crisps with chilli salt mixture.

note Kumara requires longer frying than other sweet potato varieties. For best results, deep-fry kumara separately first.

spinach and fetta pinwheels

SPINACH AND FETTA PINWHEELS

prep & cook time 30 minutes makes 24 nutritional count per pinwheel 2.1g total fat (1.1g saturated); 125kJ (30 cal); 0.6g carbohydrate; 2.1g protein; 0.5g fibre

250g frozen spinach, thawed
100g fetta cheese, crumbled
½ cup (40g) grated parmesan cheese
2 sheets puff pastry
1 egg

1 Preheat oven to 220°C/200°C fan-forced. Oil oven trays; line with baking paper.
2 Squeeze excess moisture from spinach. Chop spinach coarsely; pat dry between sheets of absorbent paper.
3 Sprinkle spinach and combined cheeses over pastry sheets; season. Roll pastry tightly to enclose filling. Cut each roll into 12 slices.
4 Place pinwheels, cut-side up, on trays; brush with a little egg. Bake about 15 minutes or until browned lightly.

Soak skewers in water for 30 minutes prior to using to prevent them from scorching during cooking.

LEMON, GARLIC AND OREGANO LAMB SKEWERS

prep & cook time **30 minutes (+ refrigeration)** makes **16** nutritional count per skewer **2.9g total fat (1g saturated fat); 284kJ (68 cal); 0g carbohydrate; 10.3g protein; 0g fibre**

Cut 800g lamb fillets into 2cm pieces. Combine lamb in medium bowl with 1 tablespoon olive oil, 2 teaspoons finely grated lemon rind, 1 clove crushed garlic and 2 tablespoons finely chopped fresh oregano; season. Cover; refrigerate 1 hour. Stir in 1 tablespoon lemon juice. Thread lamb onto 16 small bamboo skewers or strong toothpicks; cook skewers on heated oiled grill plate (or grill or barbecue) until cooked through.

VEGIE AND HALOUMI SKEWERS

prep & cook time **35 minutes** makes **16** nutritional count per skewer **26.2g total fat (4g saturated fat); 1296kJ (310 cal); 15.6g carbohydrate; 3.4g protein; 0.7g fibre**

Cut 180g haloumi cheese into 16 x 2cm cubes; cut 1 small red capsicum into 2cm pieces. Cut 1 large zucchini in half lengthways; cut each half into eight 2cm pieces. Thread haloumi, capsicum and zucchini onto 16 small bamboo skewers or strong toothpicks. Cook skewers on heated oiled grill plate (or barbecue) until tender. Meanwhile, combine ½ cup mayonnaise, 1 tablespoon lime juice and 2 teaspoons harissa in small bowl; season to taste. Serve skewers with lime and harissa mayonnaise.

GRILLED FISH KEBABS

prep & cook time **30 minutes** makes **8** nutritional count
per kebab **4g total fat (1.6g saturated fat); 706kJ
(169 cal); 4.3g carbohydrate; 28.1g protein; 1.3g fibre**

Cut 1kg firm white fish fillets, 2 medium zucchini
and 1 medium red capsicum into similar-sized
chunks; cut 1 medium red onion into wedges.
Thread ingredients onto eight bamboo skewers.
Cook skewers on heated oiled grill plate (or grill
or barbecue) about 10 minutes. Meanwhile,
combine 1 cup yogurt, 2 tablespoons lemon
juice, 3 crushed garlic cloves, 2 teaspoons each
ground cumin and coriander, and 1 teaspoon
sweet paprika in small bowl; season to taste.
Serve skewers topped with yogurt mixture;
sprinkle with ½ cup loosely packed fresh
coriander leaves.

note **We used thick-cut ling fillets in this recipe.**

SUMAC AND SESAME CHICKEN SKEWERS

prep & cook time **30 minutes** makes **16** nutritional count
per skewer **2.6g total fat (0.7g saturated fat); 222kJ
(53 cal); 0g carbohydrate; 8.1g protein; 0g fibre**

Cut 600g chicken breast fillets into 2cm cubes;
thread onto 16 small bamboo skewers or strong
toothpicks. Combine 1 tablespoon sumac,
1 teaspoon sesame seeds and 1 teaspoon
black sesame seeds in small bowl; season.
Sprinkle sumac mixture all over skewers. Cook
skewers on heated oiled grill plate (or grill or
barbecue) until chicken is cooked through.
Serve with lemon wedges.

CHICKEN GOW GEES

prep & cook time 30 minutes serves 6 nutritional count
per serving 1g total fat (0.3g saturated fat); 201kJ
(48 cal); 1g carbohydrate; 8g protein; 0.4g fibre

200g chicken breast fillet, minced
1 cup (80g) finely shredded wombok
1cm piece fresh ginger (5g), grated
1 clove garlic, crushed
1 tablespoon japanese soy sauce
2 teaspoons mirin
¼ teaspoon ground white pepper
2 green onions, sliced thinly
1 tablespoon coarsely chopped fresh
   coriander leaves
18 gow gee wrappers
chilli dipping sauce
2 tablespoons rice vinegar
1 fresh long red chilli, sliced thinly

1 Combine mince, wombok, ginger, garlic,
sauce, mirin, pepper, onion and coriander in
medium bowl; season.
2 Divide mince mixture evenly among gow gee
wrappers. Brush edges of wrappers with water;
pinch points of wrappers together to completely
enclose filling. Pleat edge of wrappers to seal.
3 Place gow gees in baking-paper-lined large
bamboo steamer; cover tightly. Steam over
large saucepan of boiling water about 8 minutes
or until gow gees are cooked through.
4 Meanwhile, make chilli dipping sauce.
5 Serve gow gees with sauce.
chilli dipping sauce Combine ingredients in
small bowl.

note You can buy 200g chicken mince instead of
mincing your own, if you prefer.

FRIED FISH SANDWICHES

prep & cook time **30 minutes** makes **12** nutritional count per slice 4.2g total fat (1.1g saturated fat); 673kJ (161 cal); 19.5g carbohydrate; 10.1g protein; 1.8g fibre

2 cloves garlic, unpeeled
½ cup (140g) greek-style yogurt
¼ cup finely chopped fresh mint
8 small white fish fillets (320g), skin on
2 tablespoons plain flour
2 teaspoons smoked paprika
1 teaspoon ground cumin
1 tablespoon olive oil
1 loaf turkish bread (430g), split, toasted
1 baby cos lettuce, leaves separated
2 medium tomatoes (300g), sliced thinly
½ small red onion (50g), sliced thinly

1 Preheat oven to 200°C/180°C fan-forced.
2 Place garlic on oven tray; roast, uncovered, about 10 minutes or until soft. Cool; peel garlic.
3 Blend or process garlic and yogurt until smooth; stir in mint. Season.
4 Coat fish in combined flour and spices; shake off excess. Heat oil in large frying pan; cook fish, both sides, until browned and crisp.
5 Spread yogurt over one half of bread; top with lettuce, tomato, onion, fish and remaining bread. Cut into 12 slices.

note We used sand whiting fillets in this recipe.

fruit and coconut trail mix

FRUIT AND COCONUT TRAIL MIX

prep & cook time 25 minutes (+ cooling) makes 3 cups
nutritional count per ⅓ cup 11.8g total fat
(2.5g saturated fat); 869kJ (208 cal);
20.7g carbohydrate; 4.2g protein; 3.7g fibre

2 tablespoons honey
2 teaspoons olive oil
¼ teaspoon mixed spice
½ cup (70g) pistachios
½ cup (80g) almond kernels
½ cup (25g) toasted flaked coconut
½ cup (65g) dried cranberries
½ cup (75g) coarsely chopped dried apricots
½ cup (70g) coarsely chopped dried dates

1 Preheat oven to 180°C/160°C fan-forced.
2 Combine honey, oil and spice in small bowl.
3 Combine nuts in shallow baking dish; drizzle
with honey mixture. Roast, uncovered, about
10 minutes or until browned lightly, stirring
halfway through cooking time. Cool 15 minutes.
4 Stir in remaining ingredients; cool.

HAM AND CHEESE PINWHEELS

prep & cook time 1 hour makes 12 nutritional count
per pinwheel 7.5g total fat (3.9g saturated fat); 865kJ
(207 cal); 20.8g carbohydrate; 12.3g protein; 1.2g fibre

6 eggs, beaten lightly
2 cups (300g) self-raising flour
1 tablespoon caster sugar
30g butter
¾ cup (180ml) low-fat milk
¼ cup (70g) tomato paste
175g shaved ham, cut into thin strips
1 cup (120g) grated reduced-fat
    cheddar cheese

1 Preheat oven to 200°C/180°C fan-forced.
Oil 19cm x 29cm rectangular slice pan.
2 Cook egg in oiled medium frying pan over
low heat, stirring constantly, until scrambled.
3 Sift flour and sugar into medium bowl; rub in
butter. Stir in milk; mix to a soft, sticky dough.
Knead dough on floured surface; roll dough
into 30cm x 40cm rectangle.
4 Spread tomato paste over dough; sprinkle
with ham, top with egg then sprinkle with
cheese. Season.
5 Starting from long side, roll dough up firmly;
trim ends. Cut roll into 12 slices; place pinwheels,
cut-side up, in single layer, in pan. Bake about
30 minutes. Serve warm or cold.

ham and cheese pinwheels

CARAWAY BREADSTICKS WITH BEETROOT DIP

prep & cook time **40 minutes** serves **4** nutritional count
per serving **1.1g** total fat (0.1g saturated fat); 698kJ
(167 cal); 32g carbohydrate; 5.7g protein; 2.6g fibre

¼ teaspoon dried yeast
½ cup (125ml) warm water
pinch sugar
1 cup (150g) plain flour
½ teaspoon fine (table) salt
2 teaspoons caraway seeds
cooking-oil spray
½ teaspoon sea salt flakes
beetroot dip
½ x 450g can baby beetroot, drained
¼ cup (70g) low-fat natural yogurt
1 clove garlic, crushed
2 teaspoons water

1 Preheat oven to 200°C/180°C fan-forced.
Line two oven trays with baking paper.
2 Sprinkle yeast over the water in small heatproof
jug, add sugar; stir until combined. Stand in
warm place about 10 minutes or until frothy.
3 Sift flour and fine salt into medium bowl; stir
in seeds and yeast mixture. Knead dough on
floured surface about 5 minutes or until smooth.
4 Divide dough into 16 pieces. Roll each piece
on floured surface into 15cm-long stick. Place
sticks on trays; spray lightly with oil, sprinkle
with sea salt. Bake about 15 minutes or until
browned lightly.
5 Meanwhile, make beetroot dip.
6 Serve breadsticks with beetroot dip.
beetroot dip Process ingredients until
smooth; season to taste.

notes Store breadsticks in an airtight container for up to
one week; re-crisp in the oven for a few minutes. Store
the dip, covered, in the refrigerator for up to one week.
Substitute poppy or cumin seeds for the caraway seeds.

Serve dips with garlic pizza wedges, lavosh, pitta crisps or crusty bread.

ROASTED CAPSICUM AND WALNUT DIP

prep & cook time 40 minutes makes 2 cups nutritional count per teaspoon 1.3g total fat (0.6g saturated fat); 59kJ (14 cal); 0.2g carbohydrate; 0.4g protein; 0.1g fibre

Preheat oven to 220°C/200°C fan-forced. Quarter 2 medium red capsicums; discard seeds and membranes. Roast, skin-side up, until skin blisters and blackens. Cover capsicum with plastic or paper for 5 minutes; peel away skin, then chop coarsely. Blend or process capsicum and 250g cream cheese until smooth; stir in ½ cup finely chopped roasted walnuts. Season to taste.

note Cook capsicum under a very hot grill until skins blackens, rather than in the oven, if you like, or buy char-grilled capsicum from the deli or in jars from the supermarket.

CHUNKY OLIVE AND HERB DIP

prep time 20 minutes makes 1½ cups nutritional count per teaspoon 1.6g total fat (0.2g saturated fat); 67kJ (16 cal); 0.3g carbohydrate; 0.1g protein; 0.1g fibre

Combine ½ cup finely chopped seeded green olives, ½ cup each of finely chopped fresh flat-leaf parsley and mint, ¼ cup finely chopped fresh dill, 6 drained and finely chopped anchovy fillets, 2 teaspoons finely grated lemon rind, ¼ cup lemon juice and ½ cup olive oil in medium bowl; season to taste.

DIPS

ROASTED FENNEL DIP

prep & cook time **45 minutes** makes **1½ cups** nutritional count per teaspoon **1.6g total fat (0.9g saturated fat); 67kJ (16 cal); 0.2g carbohydrate; 0.1g protein; 0.1g fibre**

Preheat oven to 200°C/180°C fan-forced. Halve 4 baby fennel bulbs with fronds lengthways; remove and discard cores. Reserve 2 teaspoons coarsely chopped fennel fronds. Combine fennel, 2 unpeeled garlic cloves and 1 tablespoon olive oil in small baking dish; roast, uncovered, about 30 minutes or until fennel is tender. Cool. Peel garlic; blend or process fennel, garlic and 1 cup sour cream until smooth. Season to taste; serve dip sprinkled with reserved fennel fronds.

WHITE BEAN DIP

prep & cook time **25 minutes** makes **2½ cups** nutritional count per teaspoon **1.2g total fat (0.7g saturated fat); 59kJ (14 cal); 0.4g carbohydrate; 0.2g protein; 0.2g fibre**

Heat 1 tablespoon olive oil in small frying pan; cook 1 thinly sliced medium leek, stirring, about 10 minutes or until leek softens. Cool. Blend or process leek, 400g can rinsed and drained white beans, 300ml cream, 1 teaspoon finely grated lemon rind and 1 tablespoon lemon juice until smooth. Stir in 2 tablespoons finely chopped fresh flat-leaf parsley; season to taste.

note **We used cannellini beans in this recipe but use any white bean you like.**

CRAB, FENNEL AND HERB QUICHE

prep & cook time 50 minutes makes 12 nutritional count per quiche 27.1g total fat (15g saturated fat); 1509kJ (361 cal); 20.3g carbohydrate; 9g protein; 1.3g fibre

3 sheets ready-rolled shortcrust pastry
1 tablespoon olive oil
1 medium fennel bulb (300g), sliced thinly
   (see notes)
250g crab meat
2 tablespoons finely chopped fennel fronds
2 tablespoons finely chopped fresh
   flat-leaf parsley
½ cup (60g) grated cheddar cheese
quiche filling
300ml cream
¼ cup (60ml) milk
3 eggs

1 Preheat oven to 200°C/180°C fan-forced. Grease 12-hole (⅓-cup/80ml) muffin pan.
2 Cut 12 x 9cm rounds from pastry; press into pan holes.
3 Heat oil in large frying pan; cook fennel, stirring, about 5 minutes or until fennel softens and browns slightly. Divide fennel among pastry cases; top with combined crab, fronds, parsley and cheese.
4 Make quiche filling.
5 Pour quiche filling into pastry cases. Bake about 25 minutes. Stand in pan 5 minutes before serving with lime wedges.
quiche filling Whisk ingredients in large jug.

notes Reserve fennel fronds when slicing the bulb. We used lump crab meat from the fish market.

baby pea and fetta rice cakes

BABY PEA AND FETTA RICE CAKES

prep & cook time 45 minutes serves 4 nutritional count per serving 11.2g total fat (5.2g saturated fat); 1041kJ (249 cal); 22.1g carbohydrate; 14.3g protein; 1.5g fibre

½ cup (100g) white long-grain rice
⅔ cup (80g) frozen baby green peas, thawed
2 tablespoons finely chopped fresh
    flat-leaf parsley
4 eggs, beaten lightly
2 tablespoons milk
80g fetta cheese, crumbled

1 Preheat oven to 180°C/160°C fan-forced. Oil eight holes of 12-hole (½-cup/125ml) oval friand pan; line bases with baking paper.
2 Cook rice in saucepan of boiling water until tender. Drain, rinse under cold water; drain well.
3 Combine rice and remaining ingredients in medium bowl; season. Divide mixture into pan holes; bake 25 minutes.
4 Stand rice cakes in pan 5 minutes before turning, top-side up, onto wire rack to cool.

sticky apricot chicken wings

STICKY APRICOT CHICKEN WINGS

prep & cook time 45 minutes (+ cooling) makes 8 nutritional count per serving 5.6g total fat (1.4g saturated fat); 606kJ (145 cal); 9.2g carbohydrate; 14.5g protein; 0.2g fibre

⅓ cup (110g) apricot jam
1 teaspoon sweet paprika
2 tablespoons lemon juice
1 tablespoon olive oil
8 large chicken wings (800g)

1 Preheat oven to 200°C/180°C fan-forced.
2 Combine jam, paprika, juice and oil in large bowl; add wings, coat all over with jam mixture.
3 Place undrained wings, in single layer, in large baking dish. Roast, uncovered, about 35 minutes or until cooked through. Serve hot or cold.

LEMON GRASS AND BEEF RICE PAPER ROLLS

prep & cook time **30 minutes** makes **12** nutritional count
per roll 1.3g total fat (0.3g saturated fat); 230kJ
(55 cal); 5.6g carbohydrate; 4.5g protein; 1.1g fibre

cooking-oil spray
180g beef fillet, minced finely
227g can water chestnuts, rinsed, drained,
    sliced thinly
10cm stick fresh lemon grass (20g),
    chopped finely
2 green onions, sliced thinly
1 fresh long red chilli, sliced thinly
1 tablespoon lemon juice
1 tablespoon kecap manis
1 tablespoon fish sauce
12 x 21cm rice paper rounds
12 large fresh mint leaves
1½ cups (120g) bean sprouts
12 sprigs fresh coriander
lemon chilli dipping sauce
¼ cup (60ml) sweet chilli sauce
2 tablespoons lemon juice

1 Make lemon chilli dipping sauce.
2 Spray medium heated frying pan with oil.
Cook mince, stirring, about 5 minutes or until
browned. Stir in chestnuts, lemon grass, onion,
chilli, juice, kecap manis and sauce. Season to
taste; cool.
3 Place 1 sheet of rice paper in medium bowl
of warm water until just softened; lift sheet
carefully from water, placing it on a clean tea
towel. Top with one mint leaf, one heaped
tablespoon of mince mixture, some of the
sprouts and a coriander sprig. Fold and roll
to enclose filling. Repeat to make a total of
12 rolls.
4 Serve with lemon chilli dipping sauce.
lemon chilli dipping sauce Combine
ingredients in small bowl.

notes You can use 180g low-fat beef mince rather than
mincing your own.
If not serving rolls immediately, place, seam-side down,
on a plastic-wrap-lined tray; cover with damp paper
towel and refrigerate until ready to serve.

lamb fritters with spicy yogurt

LAMB FRITTERS WITH SPICY YOGURT

prep & cook time 30 minutes serves 4 nutritional count per serving 49.2g total fat (13.3g saturated fat); 3511kJ (840 cal); 60.3g carbohydrate; 37.6g protein; 3g fibre

2 teaspoons ground cumin
1 cup (280g) greek-style yogurt
1 egg
1¾ cups (260g) self-raising flour
1½ cups (375ml) buttermilk
150g piece pumpkin, grated finely
2 green onions, chopped finely
300g roast lamb, chopped coarsely
vegetable oil, for shallow-frying

1 Dry-fry cumin in large frying pan, stirring, until fragrant. Combine yogurt with half the cumin in small bowl.
2 Combine egg, flour and buttermilk in large bowl with pumpkin, onion, lamb and remaining cumin; mix well. Season.
3 Heat oil in same pan; shallow-fry ¼-cups of batter, in batches, until fritters are browned lightly. Drain on absorbent paper; serve with yogurt.

roasted cherry tomato and parmesan dip

ROASTED CHERRY TOMATO AND PARMESAN DIP

prep & cook time 35 minutes serves 6 nutritional count per serving 12.6g total fat (6.9g saturated fat); 932kJ (223 cal); 20g carbohydrate; 6.4g protein; 2.4g fibre

250g cherry tomatoes
2 teaspoons olive oil
½ cup (120g) sour cream
½ cup (40g) grated parmesan cheese
2 tablespoons finely chopped fresh basil
½ teaspoon dried chilli flakes
1 stick sourdough bread (200g), sliced thinly
2 cloves garlic, halved

1 Preheat oven to 220°C/200°C fan-forced.
2 Combine tomatoes and oil on oven tray. Roast, uncovered, about 15 minutes or until tomato skins split. Cool 10 minutes.
3 Combine tomatoes, sour cream, cheese, basil and chilli in medium bowl; season.
4 Toast bread both sides. Rub garlic onto toasts; serve with tomato and parmesan dip.

TOMATO AND BACON SCROLLS

prep & cook time **40 minutes** makes **12** nutritional count per scroll **11g** total fat (5.4g saturated fat); 903kJ (216 cal); 19g carbohydrate; 9.8g protein; 1.1g fibre

2 cups (300g) self-raising flour
1 tablespoon caster sugar
50g cold butter, chopped coarsely
¾ cup (180ml) milk
¼ cup (65g) sun-dried tomato pesto
1 cup (120g) pizza cheese
3 rindless bacon rashers (210g),
    chopped finely
2 tablespoons finely chopped fresh chives

1 Preheat oven to 200°C/180°C fan-forced. Oil shallow 22cm-square cake pan.
2 Sift flour and sugar into medium bowl; rub in butter. Add milk; mix to a soft, sticky dough. Turn dough onto floured surface; knead lightly until dough is smooth. Roll dough into a 30cm x 40cm rectangle.
3 Spread dough with pesto, sprinkle with combined cheese, bacon and chives; season. Roll dough tightly from long side. Using serrated knife, trim ends. Cut roll into 12 slices; place scrolls, cut-side up, in pan. Bake scrolls about 25 minutes.

honey, soy and sesame chicken wings

HONEY, SOY AND SESAME CHICKEN WINGS

prep & cook time **45 minutes** (+ refrigeration) serves **4** nutritional count per serving **10.3g** total fat (3g saturated fat); 1233kJ (295 cal); 12.6g carbohydrate; 37.4g protein; 0.4g fibre

1kg chicken wings
¼ cup (60ml) japanese soy sauce
2 tablespoons honey
1 clove garlic, crushed
2cm piece fresh ginger (10g), grated
2 teaspoons sesame seeds
1 teaspoon sesame oil

1 Cut chicken wings into three pieces at joints; discard tips. Combine sauce, honey, garlic, ginger, seeds and oil in large bowl with chicken; season. Cover; refrigerate 3 hours or overnight.
2 Preheat oven to 220°C/200°C fan-forced.
3 Place chicken, in single layer, on oiled wire rack over large shallow baking dish; brush remaining marinade over chicken. Roast about 30 minutes or until chicken is cooked.

tomato and bacon scrolls

SAUSAGE ROLLS

prep & cook time 50 minutes makes 48 nutritional count
per sausage roll 7.1g total fat (1.9g saturated fat); 426kJ
(102 cal); 6.6g carbohydrate; 3.1g protein; 0.6g fibre

4 sheets puff pastry
1 egg, beaten lightly
mince filling
750g sausage mince
1 medium white onion (150g), chopped finely
1 cup (70g) stale breadcrumbs
1 teaspoon dried mixed herbs
1 egg, beaten lightly

1 Preheat oven to 200°C/180°C fan-forced.
Grease two oven trays.
2 Combine mince filling ingredients in large
bowl; season.
3 Cut each sheet of pastry in half. Spoon filling
into piping bag. Pipe filling along one long side
of each pastry sheet. Brush opposite edge of
pastry with egg; roll up pastry from filled edge
to enclose filling.
4 Cut into 6 even pieces, place on trays. Brush
with egg; cut small slits in top of each roll. Bake
about 25 minutes or until well browned.

note Sausage rolls can be frozen, cooked or uncooked,
for two months. Reheat frozen cooked sausage rolls
in moderate oven about 25 minutes, or cook frozen
uncooked sausage rolls in moderate oven about
45 minutes.

LAMB PITTA POCKETS WITH BABA GHANOUSH

prep & cook time 20 minutes serves 8 nutritional count per serving 7.7g total fat (2.5g saturated fat); 895kJ (214 cal); 18.6g carbohydrate; 16.5g protein; 1.8g fibre

Combine 500g lamb backstrap, 1 teaspoon finely grated lemon rind, 1 tablespoon za'atar and 1 tablespoon olive oil in medium bowl; season. Cook lamb in heated, oiled large frying pan over high heat until cooked to your liking. Cover lamb; stand 10 minutes then slice thinly. Spread inside of 4 pocket pitta breads with 250g baba ghanoush; fill with lamb and 50g baby rocket leaves.

note Baba ghanoush is a roasted eggplant (aubergine) dip or spread. It is available from delicatessens and most supermarkets.

EGG, CHEESE AND CHORIZO PANINI

prep & cook time 20 minutes makes 8 nutritional count per serving 39.9g total fat (12.6g saturated fat); 3018kJ (722 cal); 60.2g carbohydrate; 28.9g protein; 4.1g fibre

Cook 3 thickly sliced smoked chorizo sausages in heated oiled large frying pan, in batches, until browned. Drain on absorbent paper. Combine 1 cup mayonnaise and ½ teaspoon smoked paprika in small bowl; season to taste. Split 8 panini rolls in half; spread mayonnaise mixture over roll halves. Top with chorizo, 5 thinly sliced hard-boiled eggs, 80g baby spinach leaves, 150g shaved manchego cheese and remaining panini half.

notes Panini are just flat bread rolls; use whatever type of bread roll you like.
Manchego cheese is Spanish; it is available from specialist cheese stores and Spanish delicatessens. If you can't find it, use parmesan cheese instead. Use a vegetable peeler to shave the cheese.

SANDWICHES & ROLLS

CHICKEN, ALMOND AND TARRAGON MINI ROLLS

prep time **20 minutes** makes **12** nutritional count per roll **5.7g** total fat (0.7g saturated fat); **660kJ** (158 cal); 17.5g carbohydrate; 8.2g protein; 1.7g fibre

Combine 200g cooked finely shredded chicken breast fillet, ⅓ cup finely chopped fresh tarragon, ¼ cup roasted slivered almonds, 1 finely chopped trimmed celery stalk, 3 finely chopped green onions and ⅓ cup mayonnaise in medium bowl. Make a cut in tops of 12 mini bread rolls. Spoon chicken mixture into bread rolls.

note **Chicken mixture can be made one day ahead; keep, covered, in the refrigerator.**

PRAWN CANTINAS

prep & cook time **15 minutes** makes **6** nutritional count per roll **6.1g** total fat (1g saturated fat); **844kJ** (202 cal); 18g carbohydrate; 17.8g protein; 1.6g fibre

Shell and devein 18 uncooked medium king prawns. Combine prawns, 2 tablespoons lemon juice, 1 tablespoon olive oil and 1 teaspoon sweet smoked paprika in medium bowl. Cook prawn mixture in large frying pan, stirring, about 3 minutes. Cut slits in top of 6 bap rolls or other small bread rolls. Combine 120g rocket, ⅓ cup buttermilk, 1 tablespoon mayonnaise and 2 crushed garlic cloves in medium bowl; season. Divide rocket mixture between rolls; top with warm prawn mixture.

barbecued chicken mini pizzas

GOAT'S CHEESE, SPINACH AND CAPSICUM TARTS

prep & cook time **30 minutes** (+ cooling) makes **8**
nutritional count per tart **14.4g total fat**
(3g saturated fat); 849kJ (203 cal);
12.4g carbohydrate; 5.3g protein; 2g fibre

2 sheets ready-rolled puff pastry
4 large pieces roasted red capsicum (300g)
250g packet chopped frozen spinach, thawed
120g goat's cheese, crumbled
1 tablespoon olive oil
2 tablespoons basil pesto

1 Preheat oven to 220°C/200°C fan-forced. Line oven trays with baking paper.
2 Cut 8 x 9cm rounds from pastry; crimp edges of rounds to make borders; place on oven trays.
3 Cut capsicum pieces into rounds to fit inside pastry leaving a 5mm border. Finely chop remaining capsicum.
4 Squeeze excess moisture from spinach. Top capsicum with spinach, cheese and chopped capsicum; drizzle with oil. Season.
5 Bake tarts about 15 minutes. Cool; top tarts with pesto.

note **Buy roasted capsicum from the deli.**

BARBECUED CHICKEN MINI PIZZAS

prep & cook time **30 minutes** makes **8** nutritional count per pizza **5.4g total fat** (2.5g saturated fat); 443kJ (106 cal); 5.8g carbohydrate; 8.5g protein; 0.3g fibre

2 sheets puff pastry
¼ cup (60ml) barbecue sauce
1 cup (160g) shredded barbecued chicken
⅓ cup (80g) drained, coarsely chopped roasted red capsicum
1 green onion, sliced thinly
1 cup (100g) pizza cheese

1 Preheat oven to 200°C/180°C fan-forced. Oil oven trays.
2 Cut 8 x 11.5cm rounds from pastry; place on trays.
3 Spread rounds with sauce; top with chicken, capsicum, onion and cheese. Season. Bake about 15 minutes or until browned.

goat's cheese, spinach and capsicum tarts

PRAWNS WITH GARLIC AND CORNICHON MAYONNAISE

prep & cook time 15 minutes serves 8 nutritional count
per serving 19.9g total fat (3g saturated fat); 1007kJ
(241 cal); 2g carbohydrate; 13.7g protein; 0.4g fibre

24 cooked medium king prawns (1kg)
garlic and cornichon mayonnaise
2 egg yolks
3 teaspoons dijon mustard
2 tablespoons lemon juice
2 cloves garlic
pinch caster sugar
⅔ cup (160ml) light olive oil
¼ cup (45g) finely chopped cornichons
¼ cup coarsely chopped fresh
   flat-leaf parsley

1 Make garlic and cornichon mayonnaise.
2 Shell and devein prawns leaving tails intact.
3 Serve prawns with mayonnaise for dipping.
garlic and cornichon mayonnaise Blend or
process egg yolks, mustard, juice, garlic and
sugar. With motor operating, add oil in a thin
steady stream until mayonnaise is thick. Stir in
cornichons and parsley; season to taste.

note Cornichons, also known as baby gherkins, are a
very small variety of pickled cucumber; when pickled
with dill they are known as a dill pickle. Baby gherkins
are available from major supermarkets and delicatessens.

cheese scones

CHEESE SCONES

prep & cook time 35 minutes makes 8 nutritional count per scone 8.6g total fat (5.5g saturated fat); 794kJ (190 cal); 21.1g carbohydrate; 6.2g protein; 1.1g fibre

1½ cups (225g) self-raising flour
50g butter, chopped coarsely
⅓ cup (40g) grated cheddar cheese
⅓ cup (25g) grated parmesan cheese
¼ teaspoon cayenne pepper
¾ cup (180ml) buttermilk

1 Preheat oven to 220°C/200°C fan-forced. Oil shallow 20cm-round cake pan.
2 Sift flour into large bowl; rub in butter. Stir in cheddar, half the parmesan and all the cayenne pepper.
3 Add buttermilk to flour mixture; use a knife to cut buttermilk through the mixture to make a soft, sticky dough. Turn dough onto floured surface; knead lightly until smooth.
4 Press dough into an even 2cm thickness. Dip 5.5cm-round cutter into flour; cut as many rounds as possible from dough. Place scones, side by side, just touching, in pan.
5 Gently knead scraps of dough together; repeat pressing and cutting of dough, place in pan. Sprinkle tops with remaining parmesan cheese. Bake about 20 minutes.

mini cabanossi pizzas

MINI CABANOSSI PIZZAS

prep & cook time 20 minutes makes 12 nutritional count per pizza 5.1g total fat (2.1g saturated fat); 644kJ (154 cal); 19.6g carbohydrate; 6.5g protein; 1.5g fibre

440g pizza base with sauce
1 medium zucchini (120g), grated coarsely
100g cabanossi, sliced thinly
12 cherry bocconcini cheese (130g)

1 Preheat oven to 220°C/200°C fan-forced. Line oven tray with baking paper.
2 Cut 12 x 6.5cm fluted rounds from pizza base; place on tray.
3 Top pizza rounds with cabanossi, torn pieces of cheese and zucchini; season. Bake about 5 minutes or until heated through.

SPINACH AND CORN PASTIES

prep & cook time 1 hour makes 6 nutritional count
per pastie 27.1g total fat (12.6g saturated fat); 2291kJ
(548 cal); 62.7g carbohydrate; 9.8g protein; 7.5g fibre

1 tablespoon vegetable oil
2 medium potatoes (400g), cut into
  1cm pieces
1 small brown onion (80g), chopped finely
250g frozen spinach, thawed, drained
2 x 310g cans creamed corn
3 sheets shortcrust pastry
2 tablespoons milk

1 Heat half the oil in large frying pan; cook
potato, stirring, until browned lightly. Add onion;
cook, stirring, until soft. Combine potato, onion,
spinach and corn in large bowl; season.
2 Preheat oven to 200°C/180°C fan-forced.
Oil two oven trays.
3 Cut pastry sheets in half diagonally. Divide
filling among triangles, placing on one side; fold
pastry in half to enclose filling, pressing edges
with fork to seal.
4 Place pasties on trays; brush with milk. Bake
about 30 minutes or until browned lightly. Serve
with sweet chilli sauce.

CHICKEN SAUSAGE ROLLS

prep & cook time **45 minutes** makes **60** nutritional count per serving **4.8g total fat (2.2g saturated fat); 359kJ (86 cal); 6g carbohydrate; 4.5g protein; 0.5g fibre**

1kg chicken mince
1 medium brown onion (150g), chopped finely
½ cup (35g) stale breadcrumbs
1 egg
¼ cup finely chopped fresh basil
½ cup (75g) drained semi-dried tomatoes
   in oil, chopped finely
2 tablespoons tomato paste
5 sheets puff pastry
1 egg, extra

1 Preheat oven to 220°C/200°C fan-forced. Line oven trays with baking paper.

2 Combine mince, onion, breadcrumbs, egg, basil, semi-dried tomato and paste in large bowl; season.

3 Cut pastry sheets in half lengthways. Place equal amounts of chicken filling mixture lengthways down one long edge of each pastry piece; roll pastry to enclose filling. Cut each roll into six pieces; place rolls, seam-side down, on trays. Brush with extra egg; bake about 30 minutes.

4 Serve rolls hot, with tomato sauce or sweet chilli sauce.

note **You can replace the chicken mince with the same quantity of pork or beef mince.**

CLUB SANDWICH

prep & cook time 20 minutes makes 4 nutritional count
per sandwich 36.1g total fat (7.7g saturated fat); 3210kJ
(768 cal); 69.9g carbohydrate; 37.7g protein; 6.3g fibre

4 rindless bacon rashers (260g), halved
1 medium avocado (250g)
2 teaspoons lime juice
½ cup (150g) mayonnaise
12 slices white bread (540g)
12 large butter lettuce leaves
3 small tomatoes (270g), sliced thinly
150g shaved turkey breast

1 Cook bacon in heated oiled large frying pan
until crisp.
2 Mash avocado and juice in small bowl until
smooth; season.
3 Spread mayonnaise over bread slices; top
four slices with half the avocado mixture,
lettuce, tomato, turkey and bacon. Top each
with another slice of bread, mayonnaise-side
down, spread top with a little more mayonnaise.
Repeat layers with remaining fillings and bread.
Cut into triangles; use toothpicks or skewers to
hold layers in place.

CHEESE AND VEGIE SANDWICHES

prep time 20 minutes makes 4 nutritional count per
sandwich 29.2g total fat (13g saturated fat); 2190kJ
(524 cal); 45.6g carbohydrate; 17g protein; 6g fibre

Coarsely grate 1 medium carrot and 2 small
zucchini. Combine vegetables, 2 thinly sliced
green onions, 1 cup coarsely grated cheddar
cheese and ⅓ cup mayonnaise in medium bowl.
Spread 8 slices soy and linseed sandwich
bread with 40g softened butter. Sandwich
vegetable mixture between bread slices.
Remove crusts; cut sandwiches into fingers.

notes Use your favourite mayonnaise – we like the
whole-egg variety. Use butter or your favourite spread
for the sandwiches, although this filling is moist enough
without a spread. Don't season the vegies with salt, it
will draw the moisture from the zucchini, which will
make the sandwiches soggy.

HAM, CHEESE AND TOMATO CHUTNEY WRAPS

prep time 15 minutes makes 12 nutritional count
per wrap 9.2g total fat (5.2g saturated fat); 782kJ
(187 cal); 13.9g carbohydrate; 11.7g protein; 1.2g fibre

Place 2 mountain bread slices together, spread
with rounded tablespoons of tomato chutney.
Top with 10g baby spinach leaves, ½ cup
coarsely grated cheddar cheese and 75g shaved
leg ham; season. Roll to enclose. Repeat to
make four rolls. Cut rolls into thirds crossways
to serve.

SANDWICHES & WRAPS

PRAWN AND CAPER SANDWICHES

prep time **30 minutes** makes **36** nutritional count
per triangle **2.6g** total fat (**0.3g** saturated fat); **255kJ**
(**61** cal); **7g** carbohydrate; **2.1g** protein; **0.4g** fibre

Combine 300g cooked, shelled, finely chopped
prawns, ¼ cup rinsed, drained, finely chopped
capers, 1 cup mayonnaise, 1 teaspoon sweet
paprika, ¼ cup finely chopped fresh flat-leaf
parsley and 1 crushed garlic clove in medium
bowl; season to taste. Divide prawn mixture
between 9 slices of white bread; top with
another 9 slices bread. Trim crusts; cut each
sandwich into four triangles.

TUNA SALAD SANDWICHES

prep time **15 minutes** makes **16** nutritional count
per triangle **4.2g** total fat (**0.6g** saturated fat); **487kJ**
(**116** cal); **11.7g** carbohydrate; **7.2g** protein; **1.7g** fibre

Drain and flake 425g can tuna in brine. Combine
tuna, ½ finely chopped small red capsicum,
1 thinly sliced green onion, 1 finely chopped
trimmed celery stalk and 1 teaspoon finely
chopped fresh flat-leaf parsley in medium
bowl. Stir in combined ½ cup mayonnaise,
2 teaspoons lemon juice and 1 teaspoon dijon
mustard; season to taste. Spread four multigrain
bread slices with the tuna mixture; top with
90g green oak lettuce leaves then another four
multigrain bread slices. Cut into triangles to serve.

CROQUE MADAME

prep & cook time 35 minutes serves 4 nutritional count per serving 22.7g total fat (11.9g saturated fat); 1551kJ (371 cal); 18.4g carbohydrate; 22g protein; 3g fibre

Top 4 slices wholemeal bread with 8 slices leg ham and 4 slices cheddar cheese then another 4 slices wholemeal bread. Melt 40g butter in large frying pan. Add sandwiches; toast, in batches, until browned both sides. Fry 4 eggs in same pan until cooked. Top each sandwich with an egg.

BLT

prep & cook time 15 minutes makes 4 nutritional count per blt 29.1g total fat (7.8g saturated fat); 2934kJ (702 cal); 69.2g carbohydrate; 37.8g protein; 5.2g fibre

Cook 8 rindless bacon rashers in heated oiled large frying pan until crisp. Meanwhile, toast 8 thick slices white bread both sides. Spread ⅓ cup mayonnaise over half the bread; top with 8 large butter lettuce leaves, 2 thinly sliced small tomatoes and bacon. Season; top with remaining bread.

TOMATO, SPINACH AND CHEESE MELTS

prep & cook time 15 minutes serves 4 nutritional count per serving 7.8g total fat (4.5g saturated fat); 936kJ (224 cal); 24.6g carbohydrate; 12.3g protein; 3g fibre

Preheat grill. Layer 60g baby spinach leaves, 2 thinly sliced medium tomatoes and ⅔ cup grated cheddar cheese on 4 split english muffins. Place on oven tray under preheated grill until cheese melts.

BRUSCHETTA WITH TOMATO, BASIL AND CAPERS

prep & cook time 15 minutes serves 6 nutritional count per serving 8.3g total fat (1.2g saturated fat); 1124kJ (269 cal); 38.6g carbohydrate; 7.6g protein; 4.5g fibre

Seed and finely dice 6 ripe tomatoes; combine in medium bowl with 2 tablespoons extra virgin olive oil, ¼ cup fresh baby basil leaves and 2 tablespoons rinsed, drained baby capers. Season. Cut 500g loaf ciabatta bread into 12 slices; toast slices both sides. Rub one side of each slice with the cut side of a garlic clove; place toast on platter, garlic-side up. Top toasts with tomato mixture; season and drizzle with extra olive oil.

MELTS & BRUSCHETTA

MEXICAN BAGEL MELT

prep & cook time **15 minutes** makes **4** nutritional count per melt **15.3g** total fat (6.1g saturated fat); 1179kJ (282 cal); 24.4g carbohydrate; 10.7g protein; 2.1g fibre

Split 2 bagels in half horizontally; spread 2 teaspoons chunky tomato salsa over each half. Top each bagel half with a quarter of a thickly sliced small avocado and 1 slice of tasty cheese; season. Place under preheated grill about 5 minutes or until cheese melts.

TUNA AND AVOCADO MELTS

prep & cook time **15 minutes** serves **4** nutritional count per serving **16.1g** total fat (6.4g saturated fat); 1300kJ (311 cal); 23.7g carbohydrate; 16.8g protein; 2.5g fibre

Preheat grill. Using back of fork, mash 1 medium avocado, drained 95g can tuna in spring water and 1 tablespoon lemon juice in small bowl. Spread over 4 split english muffins; sprinkle with ⅔ cup grated cheddar cheese. Season. Place on oven tray under preheated grill about 5 minutes or until cheese melts.

ANTIPASTO MELTS

prep & cook time **15 minutes** makes **4** nutritional count per melt **19.4g** total fat (6.5g saturated fat); 2307kJ (552 cal); 64.8g carbohydrate; 24.2g protein; 10.5g fibre

Preheat grill. Spread ⅓ cup sun-dried tomato pesto over 4 small pizza bases; top with 16 drained marinated artichoke quarters, 120g drained bottled char-grilled capsicum, and 1 cup grated mozzarella cheese. Season. Place on oven tray under grill about 5 minutes or until cheese melts.

SMOKED CHICKEN AND MANGO CHUTNEY BRUSCHETTA

prep & cook time **10 minutes** serves **4** nutritional count per serving **9.6g** total fat (2.4g saturated fat); 1605kJ (384 cal); 43.2g carbohydrate; 30.8g protein; 2.8g fibre

Toast 8 thick slices ciabatta bread. Spread 1 tablespoon low-fat mayonnaise over toast, then divide 400g thinly sliced smoked chicken, 40g mesclun and ⅓ cup mango chutney between toasts.

BABA GHANOUSH a roasted eggplant (aubergine) dip or spread.

BACON RASHERS also known as slices of bacon, made from pork side, cured and smoked.

BASIL an aromatic herb; there are many types, but the most commonly used is sweet, or common, basil.

BEETROOT also known as red beets or beets; firm, round root vegetable.

BICARBONATE OF SODA also known as baking or carb soda; used as a leavening agent in baking.

BREAD

bagel small ring-shaped bread roll; yeast-based but egg-less, with a dense, chewy texture and shiny crust. A true bagel is boiled in water before it's baked.

brioche rich, yeast-risen french bread made with butter and eggs. Available from pâtisseries or better bakeries.

ciabatta in Italian, the word means 'slipper', which is the traditional shape of this popular white bread with a crisp crust.

english muffins a round yeasted teacake; often confused with crumpets. Pre-baked and sold packaged in supermarkets, muffins should be split open and toasted before eating.

flatbread any non-yeasted, thin, dry, soft-textured bread; made from corn or wheat flour.

mountain bread a thin, dry, soft-textured bread, that can be used for sandwiches or rolled up and filled with your favourite filling.

pitta also known as lebanese bread. This wheat-flour pocket bread is sold in large, flat pieces that separate into two thin rounds. Also available as pocket pitta.

sourdough has a very lightly sour taste from the yeast starter culture used to make the bread. Has a dense centre and crisp crust.

turkish also known as pide; comes in long (about 45cm) flat loaves as well as individual rounds.

BREADCRUMBS stale one- or two-day-old bread made into crumbs by blending or processing.

BUTTER use salted or unsalted (sweet) butter; 125g is equal to one stick (4 ounces) of butter.

BUTTERMILK originally the term given to the slightly sour liquid left after butter was churned from cream, today it is made similarly to yogurt. Sold alongside fresh milk products in supermarkets. Despite the implication of its name, it's low in fat.

CABANOSSI a processed sausage made from pork and beef and seasoned with spices and fresh garlic. Traditionally wood smoked for its unique smoked flavour.

CAPERS the grey-green buds of a warm climate (Mediterranean) shrub, sold either dried and salted or pickled in a vinegar brine. Baby capers, those picked early, are very small, fuller-flavoured and more expensive than the full-size one. Must be rinsed well before using.

CAPSICUM also known as bell pepper or, simply, pepper. Available in many colours: red, green, yellow, orange and purplish-black. Discard seeds and membranes before use.

roasted available loose from delis or packed in jars in oil or brine.

CARAWAY available in seed or ground form; used in sweet and savoury dishes. Has a pungent aroma and a distinctly sweet but tangy flavour.

CAYENNE PEPPER long, thin, extremely hot red chilli usually sold dried and ground.

CHEESE

blue mould-treated cheeses mottled with blue veining. Includes firm and crumbly stilton types to mild, creamy brie-like cheeses.

bocconcine walnut-sized, fresh, baby mozzarella, a delicate, semi-soft, white cheese. Spoils rapidly, so must be kept under refrigeration, in brine, for one or two days at most.

brie smooth and voluptuous, brie has a bloomy white rind and a creamy centre that becomes runnier as it ripens.

cream commonly known as Philly or Philadelphia, a soft cows'-milk cheese with a fat content of at least 33%. Sold at supermarkets.

fetta a crumbly goat- or sheep-milk cheese with a sharp salty taste.

goat's made from goats' milk, has an earthy, strong taste; available in soft and firm textures, in various shapes and sizes, sometimes rolled in ash or herbs.

haloumi a firm, cream-coloured sheeps'-milk cheese matured in brine; somewhat like a minty, salty fetta in flavour. Can be grilled or fried, briefly, without breaking down. Eat while still warm as it becomes tough and rubbery on cooling.

pecorino the generic Italian name for cheeses made from sheep milk. A hard, white to pale yellow cheese. If you can't find it, use parmesan.

pizza a blend of grated mozzarella, cheddar and parmesan cheeses.

CHICKEN DRUMETTES small fleshy part of the wing between shoulder and elbow, trimmed to resemble a drumstick.

GLOSSARY

CHILLI available in many different types and sizes. Use rubber gloves when seeding and chopping fresh chillies as they can burn your skin. Removing seeds and membranes lessens the heat level.

CHIVES related to the onion and leek, with subtle onion flavour.

garlic chives also known as chinese chives; have rougher, flatter leaves than simple chives, and possess a pink-tinged teardrop-shaped flowering bud at the end; used as a salad green, or steamed and eaten as a vegetable.

CHORIZO SAUSAGE a sausage of Spanish origin, made of coarsely ground pork and highly seasoned with garlic and chilli.

CORIANDER also known as pak chee, cilantro or chinese parsley; bright-green leafy herb with a pungent flavour. Both the stems and roots of coriander are also used in Thai cooking; wash well before using. Also available ground or as seeds; these should not be substituted for fresh coriander as the tastes are completely different.

CORNFLAKES manufactured cereal made of dehydrated then baked crisp flakes of corn. Also available is a prepared finely ground mixture used for coating or crumbing food.

CORNFLOUR also known as cornstarch; used as a thickening agent. Available as 100% corn (maize) and wheaten cornflour. Maize cornflour has no gluten.

CREAM we use fresh cream, also known as pure cream and pouring cream, unless otherwise stated; it has no additives unlike commercially thickened cream. Minimum fat content 35%.

crème fraîche mature fermented cream having a slightly tangy, nutty flavour and velvety texture.

sour a thick commercially-cultured soured cream.

CUMIN a spice also known as zeera or comino; has a spicy, nutty flavour.

ENOKI MUSHROOMS also known as enokitake; grown and bought in clumps, these delicately-flavoured mushrooms have small cream caps on long thin stalks. Available from Asian food shops, greengrocers and some larger supermarkets.

FISH FILLETS, FIRM WHITE blue eye, bream, flathead, swordfish, ling, whiting, jewfish, snapper or sea perch are all good choices. Check for any small pieces of bone and use tweezers to remove them.

FLOUR

plain an all-purpose flour made from wheat.

self-raising plain flour sifted with baking powder in the proportion of 1 cup flour to 2 teaspoons baking powder.

GHEE butter that has been clarified by removing the milk solids, meaning it can reach higher temperatures than regular butter before burning.

GINGER also known as green or root ginger; the thick gnarled root of a tropical plant.

GOW GEE WRAPPERS wonton wrappers, spring roll or egg pastry sheets can be substituted.

HARISSA PASTE an extremely hot Moroccan paste made from dried chillies, cumin garlic, oil and caraway seeds. Also available as a sauce, which is slightly milder.

HERBS, DRIED MIXED a blend of dried crushed thyme, rosemary, marjoram, basil, oregano and sage.

KECAP MANIS see sauces.

KUMARA Polynesian name of an orange-fleshed sweet potato often confused with yam.

LAMB BACKSTRAP (fillet) the larger fillet from a row of loin chops.

LEBANESE CUCUMBER short, slender and thin-skinned. Probably the most popular variety because of its tender, edible skin, tiny, yielding seeds, and sweet, fresh taste.

LEMON GRASS a tall, clumping, lemon-smelling and tasting, sharp-edged grass; the white lower part of each stem is chopped and used in Asian cooking.

LEMON THYME a herb with a lemony scent. The citrus scent is enhanced by crushing the leaves in your hands before using the herb.

LETTUCE

butter small, round, loosely formed heads with buttery-textured leaves and a sweet flavour.

cos also known as romaine lettuce.

iceberg heavy, round, crisp lettuce with tightly packed leaves.

MESCLUN mixed baby salad leaves also sold as salad mix or gourmet salad mix; a mixture of young lettuce and other green leaves.

MINCE also ground meat.

MIRIN a Japanese champagne-coloured cooking wine; made of glutinous rice and alcohol and used only for cooking.

ONIONS

green also known as scallion or (incorrectly) shallot; an immature onion picked before the bulb has formed. Has long, green stalks.

shallots also called french shallots, golden shallots or eschalots; small, brown-skinned, elongated members of the onion family.

red also known as spanish, red spanish or bermuda onion; a large, sweet-flavoured, purple-red onion.

PANCETTA Italian bacon that is cured, but not smoked.

PARSLEY, FLAT-LEAF also known as continental or italian parsley.

PIZZA BASES pre-packaged for home-made pizzas. They come in a variety of sizes (snack or family) and thicknesses (thin and crispy or thick).

PRAWNS also known as shrimp.

PROSCIUTTO a kind of unsmoked Italian ham; salted, air-cured and aged, it is usually eaten uncooked.

RICE BUBBLES puffed rice breakfast cereal.

RICE PAPER SHEETS also known as banh trang. Made from rice paste and stamped into rounds. They are quite brittle and will break if dropped; dipped momentarily in water become pliable wrappers. Make good spring-roll wrappers.

ROCKET also known as arugula, rugula and rucola; a peppery-tasting green leaf. Baby rocket leaves are also available.

SAUCES

barbecue a spicy, tomato-based sauce used to marinate or baste.

fish made from pulverised salted fermented fish, most often anchovies. Has a pungent smell and strong taste; use sparingly.

soy made from fermented soya beans. Several variations are available; we use Japanese soy sauce unless indicated otherwise.

japanese soy an all-purpose low-sodium soy sauce made with more wheat content than its Chinese counterparts. Possibly the best table soy and the one to choose if you only want one variety.

kecap manis a dark, thick sweet soy sauce. Depending on the brand, the soy's sweetness is from the addition of either molasses or palm sugar when brewed.

light soy a fairly thin, pale but salty tasting sauce; used in dishes in which the natural colour of the ingredients is to be maintained. Not to be confused with salt-reduced or low-sodium soy sauces.

tomato also known as ketchup or catsup; made from tomatoes, vinegar and spices.

tomato pasta made from a blend of tomatoes, herbs and spices.

worcestershire thin, dark-brown spicy sauce made from garlic, soy sauce, tamarind, onions, molasses, anchovies and vinegar.

SHALLOTS see onions.

SPINACH also known as english spinach and, incorrectly, silver beet. Baby spinach is also available.

SUGAR

brown soft, finely granulated sugar retaining molasses for its characteristic colour and flavour.

caster also known as superfine or finely granulated table sugar.

SUMAC a purple-red, astringent spice ground from berries growing on shrubs around the Mediterranean; adds a tart, lemony flavour to food.

SWEET POTATO there are three types, kumara, or orange sweet potato, with a sweet flavour, the white sweet potato, which has a purple flesh and an earthy flavour, and the purple sweet potato, which has a white flesh that discolours when cut and is best for baking.

TARRAGON an aromatic herb with an anise-like flavour; available fresh, dried and powdered.

TURMERIC, GROUND also known as kamin; imparts a golden colour to the dishes of which it's a part.

VEGEMITE Australia's favourite spread. A dark brown food paste mainly spread on sandwiches and toast. Made from leftover brewers' yeast extract, the taste is described as salty, slightly bitter, and malty. The texture is smooth and sticky.

VINEGAR

balsamic made from grape juice; it is a deep rich brown colour with a sweet and sour flavour.

rice a colourless vinegar made from fermented rice. Also known as seasoned rice vinegar.

white made from cane sugar.

WATER CHESTNUTS resembles a chestnut in appearance, hence the English name. They are small brown tubers with a crisp, white, nutty-tasting flesh. Available both fresh and canned.

WHITE BEAN a generic term we use for canned or dried navy, cannellini, haricot or great northern beans; all of which can be substituted for each other.

WOMBOK also known as peking cabbage, chinese cabbage or petsai. Elongated in shape with pale green, crinkly leaves.

WONTON WRAPPERS also known as wonton skins; made of flour, eggs and water. Gow gee, egg or spring roll sheets can be substituted.

ZA'ATAR a blend of roasted dried spices, usually sesame seeds, wild marjoram, thyme and sumac; available in Middle-Eastern food shops and delicatessens.

ZUCCHINI (courgette) small green, yellow or white vegetable belonging to the squash family.

CONVERSION CHART

MEASURES

One Australian metric measuring cup holds approximately 250ml, one Australian metric tablespoon holds 20ml, one Australian metric teaspoon holds 5ml.

The difference between one country's measuring cups and another's is within a 2- or 3-teaspoon variance, and will not affect your cooking results. North America, New Zealand and the United Kingdom use a 15ml tablespoon. All cup and spoon measurements are level. The most accurate way of measuring dry ingredients is to weigh them. When measuring liquids, use a clear glass or plastic jug with metric markings.

We use large eggs with an average weight of 60g.

DRY MEASURES

METRIC	IMPERIAL
15g	½oz
30g	1oz
60g	2oz
90g	3oz
125g	4oz (¼lb)
155g	5oz
185g	6oz
220g	7oz
250g	8oz (½lb)
280g	9oz
315g	10oz
345g	11oz
375g	12oz (¾lb)
410g	13oz
440g	14oz
470g	15oz
500g	16oz (1lb)
750g	24oz (1½lb)
1kg	32oz (2lb)

LIQUID MEASURES

METRIC	IMPERIAL
30ml	1 fluid oz
60ml	2 fluid oz
100ml	3 fluid oz
125ml	4 fluid oz
150ml	5 fluid oz
190ml	6 fluid oz
250ml	8 fluid oz
300ml	10 fluid oz
500ml	16 fluid oz
600ml	20 fluid oz
1000ml (1 litre)	1¾ pints

LENGTH MEASURES

METRIC	IMPERIAL
3mm	⅛in
6mm	¼in
1cm	½in
2cm	¾in
2.5cm	1in
5cm	2in
6cm	2½in
8cm	3in
10cm	4in
13cm	5in
15cm	6in
18cm	7in
20cm	8in
23cm	9in
25cm	10in
28cm	11in
30cm	12in (1ft)

OVEN TEMPERATURES

These oven temperatures are only a guide for conventional ovens.
For fan-forced ovens, check the manufacturer's manual.

	°C (CELSIUS)	°F (FAHRENHEIT)	GAS MARK
Very slow	120	250	½
Slow	150	300	1-2
Moderately slow	160	325	3
Moderate	180	350	4-5
Moderately hot	200	400	6
Hot	220	425	7-8
Very hot	240	475	9

A

antipasto melts 73
avocado smash 14

B

baby pea and fetta rice cakes 47
baked ricotta 23
barbecued chicken mini pizzas 58
beef and lemon grass
  rice paper rolls 48
best-ever chicken sandwiches 11
BLT 72
blue cheese and fig bites 20
bolognese turnovers 27
breadsticks caraway 41
brie and quince matchsticks 21
bruschetta with tomato, basil
  and capers 72

C

cabanossi pizzas, mini 63
caprese tartlets 21
caramelised tomato and
  ham bites 20
caraway breadsticks with
  beetroot dip 41

cheese
  and ham pinwheels 38
  and vegie sandwiches 70
  baked ricotta 23
  blue cheese and fig bites 20
  brie and quince matchsticks 21
  fetta and spinach pinwheels 31
  goat's cheese, spinach and
    capsicum tarts 58
  scones 63
  straws, Vegemite 11
  vegie and haloumi skewers 32

chicken
  almond and tarragon
    mini rolls 57
  barbecued chicken mini pizzas 58
  drumettes, lemon pepper 14
  gow gees 34

liver pâté 17
sandwiches, best-ever 11
sausage rolls 66
skewers, sumac and
  sesame 33
teriyaki chicken rice paper rolls 28
wings, honey, soy
  and sesame 52
wings, sticky apricot 47
chilli salt prawns 4
club sandwich 69
corn cakes with avocado smash 14
crab, fennel and herb quiche 44
croque madame 72
croquettes, fish and caper 24

D

dipping sauces
  chilli 34
  lemon chilli 48
  sweet soy 7
  yogurt 4

dips
  beetroot dip 41
  chunky olive and herb dip 42
  capsicum and walnut dip,
    roasted 42
  cherry tomato and parmesan
    dip, roasted 51
  fennel dip, roasted 43
  white bean dip 43
dumplings, pork 7

E

egg, cheese and chorizo panini 56

F

fetta and baby pea rice cakes 47
fetta and spinach pinwheels 31
fig and blue cheese bites 20

fish
  and caper croquettes 24
  fried fish sandwiches 37
  kebabs, grilled 33
  sandwiches, fried 37

frittatas, pea and pancetta 18
fritters, lamb, with spicy yogurt 51
fruit and cereal snack 13
fruit and coconut trail mix 38

G

garlic and cornichon
  mayonnaise 61
goat's cheese, spinach and
  capsicum tarts 58
grilled fish kebabs 33

H

haloumi and vegie skewers 32
ham and caramelised tomato
  bites 20
ham and cheese pinwheels 38
ham, cheese and tomato chutney
  wraps 70
honey, soy and sesame chicken
  wings 52
hot and spicy popcorn 13

K

kebabs (see also skewers)
  grilled fish 33

L

lamb
  fritters with spicy yogurt 51
  pitta pockets with
    baba ghanoush 56
  skewers, lemon, garlic
    and oregano 32
lemon chilli dipping sauce 48
lemon grass and beef rice paper
  rolls 48
lemon pepper chicken
  drumettes 14
lemon, garlic and oregano lamb
  skewers 32

M

mayonnaise, garlic and
  cornichon 61
melon in prosciutto 4
mexican bagel melts 73

INDEX

mince filling 55
mini cabanossi pizzas 63
muffins, pizza 23

N

nut mix, orange and honey 12

O

olives, warm orange & fennel 12
orange and honey nut mix 12

P

pasties, spinach and corn 65
pâté, chicken liver 17
pea and pancetta frittatas 18
pea, baby, and fetta rice cakes 47
pinwheels, ham and cheese 38
pizza muffins 23
pizzas, barbecued chicken mini 58
pizzas, mini cabanossi 63
popcorn, hot and spicy 13
pork dumplings 7
potato crisps with chilli salt,
  sweet 31

prawn(s)
  and caper sandwiches 71
  cantinas 57
  cocktails 27
  with garlic and cornichon
    mayonnaise 61
  chilli salt 4
prosciutto, melon in 4

Q

quiche filling 44
quiche, crab, fennel and herb 44

R

rice cakes, baby pea and fetta 47
rice paper rolls, lemon grass
  and beef 48
rice paper rolls, teriyaki chicken 28
rice paper rolls, vegetable 8

S

sandwiches, wraps, rolls etc
  antipasto melts 73
  best-ever chicken sandwiches 11

BLT 72
bruschetta with tomato, basil
  and capers 72
caraway breadsticks 41
cheese and vegie sandwiches 70
chicken, almond and tarragon
  mini rolls 57
club sandwich 69
croque madame 72
egg, cheese and chorizo
  panini 56
fried fish sandwiches 37
ham and cheese pinwheels 38
ham, cheese and tomato
  chutney wraps 70
lamb pitta pockets with baba
  ghanoush 56
mexican bagel melts 73
prawn and caper sandwiches 71
prawn cantinas 57
smoked chicken and mango
  chutney bruschetta 73
spinach and fetta pinwheels 31
tomato and bacon scrolls 52
tomato, spinach and cheese
  melts 72
tuna and avocado melts 73
tuna salad sandwiches 71
sausage rolls 55
sausage rolls, chicken 66
scones, cheese 63
scrolls, tomato and bacon 52

seafood
  crab, fennel and herb quiche 44
  fish and caper croquettes 24
  fried fish sandwiches 37
  grilled fish kebabs 33
  prawn and caper sandwiches 71
  prawn cantinas 57
  prawn cocktails 27
  prawns with garlic and cornichon
    mayonnaise 61

tuna and avocado melts 73
tuna salad sandwiches 71
chilli salt prawns 4

skewers (see also kebab)
  lemon, garlic and oregano
    lamb skewers 32
  sumac and sesame chicken
    skewers 33
  vegie and haloumi skewers 32
smoked chicken and mango
  chutney bruschetta 73
spinach and corn pasties 65
spinach and fetta pinwheels 31
sticky apricot chicken wings 47
sumac and sesame chicken
  skewers 33
sweet potato crisps with
  chilli salt 31
sweet soy dipping sauce 7

T

tartlets, caprese 21
tarts, goat's cheese, spinach
  and capsicum 58
teriyaki chicken rice paper rolls 28
tomato and bacon scrolls 52
tomato and ham bites,
  caramelised 20
tomato, spinach and cheese
  melts 72
trail mix, fruit and coconut 38
tuna and avocado melts 73
tuna salad sandwiches 71

V

Vegemite cheese straws 11
vegetable rice paper rolls 8
vegie and haloumi skewers 32

W

warm orange & fennel olives 12

Y

yogurt dipping sauce 4

Published in 2010 by ACP Books, Sydney
ACP Books are published by ACP Magazines
a division of PBL Media Pty Limited

ACP BOOKS

General manager Christine Whiston
Editor-in-chief Susan Tomnay
Creative director Hieu Chi Nguyen
Art director Hannah Blackmore
Designer Sarah Holmes
Senior editor Wendy Bryant
Food director Pamela Clark
Food editor Rebecca Squadrito

Sales & rights director Brian Cearnes
Marketing manager Bridget Cody
Senior business analyst Rebecca Varela
Circulation manager Jama Mclean
Operations manager David Scotto
Production manager Victoria Jefferys

Published by ACP Books, a division of
ACP Magazines Ltd, 54 Park St, Sydney;
GPO Box 4088, Sydney, NSW 2001.
phone (02) 9282 8618; fax (02) 9267 9438.
acpbooks@acpmagazines.com.au;
www.acpbooks.com.au

Printed by Toppan Printing Co., China.

United Kingdom Distributed by Australian Consolidated Press (UK),
phone (01604) 642 200; fax (01604) 642 300; books@acpuk.com

Title: Snazzy snacks / food director Pamela Clark.
ISBN: 978 1 86396931 4 (pbk.)
Notes: Includes index.
Subjects: Snack foods. Cookery.
Other Authors/Contributors: Clark, Pamela.
Dewey Number: 641.539

Send recipe enquiries to: recipeenquiries@acpmagazines.com.au